The Mummy Returns

JOHN WHITMAN

Based on the motion picture screenplay written by
STEPHEN SOMMERS

Level 2

Retold by Nancy Taylor
Series Editors: Andy Hopkins and Jocelyn Potter

Pearson Education Limited
Edinburgh Gate, Harlow,
Essex CM20 2JE, England
and Associated Companies throughout the world.

ISBN 0997 805757

First published by Bantam Skylark 2001
This edition first published 2002
This edition published 2006

1 3 5 7 9 10 8 6 4 2

Typeset by Pantek Arts Ltd, Maidstone, Kent
Set in 11/14pt Bembo
Printed in China
SWTC/01

Published by Pearson Education Limited in association with Penguin
Books Ltd, both companies being subsidiaries of Pearson Plc

Contents

Introduction

People in Egypt told the story of the Scorpion King and the great pyramid of Anubis. In the Year of the Scorpion, they said, he and his soldiers will wake up. They will begin their battles again, and this time they will kill everybody and everything. Somebody has to kill the Scorpion King, or the world will end.

The Scorpion King and his soldiers are asleep under the desert of Ahm Shere. But it is now 1933, the Year of the Scorpion, and the Scorpion King is going to wake up.

Two people want to find him: Meela, a beautiful young woman, and Lock-Nah, a strong young man. They have a plan. First, they will bring Imhotep, the mummy, back to life. Then, they will follow him to Ahm Shere and take the Scorpion King's powers. Meela wants the mummy's love. Lock-Nah wants gold. Imhotep wants to be king of the world.

But, ten years after their last battle with Imhotep, Evelyn and Rick O'Connell are back in Egypt with Alex, their young son. In an old, dark temple, Evelyn O'Connell finds the Bracelet of Anubis. Lock-Nah, Meela, and Imhotep want this bracelet. It will show them the way to Ahm Shere. But the bracelet is on Alex's arm, and he can't get it off.

The Scorpion King will wake up in seven days! Who will win this battle? Who will find Ahm Shere? Will somebody stop the Scorpion King? Or, is this the end of the world?

The Mummy Returns is the second story by Stephen Sommers about the O'Connells and their exciting battles with the mummy, Imhotep. It is also a movie. In the movie, Brendan Fraser is Rick, Rachel Weisz is Evelyn, Arnold Vosloo is Imhotep, and Dwayne "The Rock" Johnson is the Scorpion King.

Chapter 1 The Scorpion King

Egypt, 4000 BC★

The tall, strong young man walks across the desert. There are a lot of dead soldiers, his soldiers, on the ground at his feet. After many great battles with the Egyptians, they will never see their homes in Akkad again. But, the Scorpion King didn't die with his men because he wears the Bracelet of Anubis on his arm.

He stops and looks up into the sky.

"I am the Scorpion King!" he shouts. "Nobody can kill me!"

He walks away into the desert of Ahm Shere.

The Scorpion King carries his knife in one hand. It feels heavy because he is very tired. Suddenly, he hears horses and looks up again. He sees thousands of Egyptian soldiers on horseback. They want to kill the great king from Akkad. They want to stop the battles. The Scorpion King is going to die. Who can help him? He looks at the sky.

"Anubis," he calls to the great god of the dead, "please, hear me! Help me today, and I will build a great pyramid of gold for you. And, I will give you my life."

The Scorpion King shouts loudly to the sky, but nobody answers him. The Egyptian soldiers are coming. His end is near.

Then he feels something on his foot. It is a scorpion! The Scorpion King laughs and puts the animal in his mouth. He eats the scorpion, and suddenly he is strong again. Around him the desert changes into green trees and blue water. Behind him he sees 10,000 soldiers with faces of dogs. They are the soldiers of Anubis, and now they are going to fight for him. Now they are *his* soldiers.

★BC: before Christ was born.

1

The Scorpion King shouts loudly to the sky, but nobody answers him.

For the next year, the Scorpion King and the dog-face soldiers move across Egypt and kill more and more Egyptians. Then at the end of the year, the Scorpion King takes the city of Thebes. Anubis is waiting for him.

"Your life is mine," says Anubis. "I want it today."

"What will happen to my soldiers?" asks the Scorpion King.

"You and these soldiers will leave this life. You will sleep for 6,000 years."

The Scorpion King feels very cold for a minute, and then he feels nothing. Nothing for 6,000 years.

◆

People in Egypt told the story of the Scorpion King and the great pyramid of Anubis. In the Year of the Scorpion, they said, he and his soldiers will wake up. They will begin their battles again, and this time they will kill everybody and everything. Somebody has to kill the Scorpion King, or the world will end.

Many people knew the story, but nobody could find the desert of Ahm Shere. Nobody could find the Scorpion King and stop him.

Chapter 2   The Bracelet of Anubis

Egypt, near Hamunaptra, the City of the Dead, 1933

Rick O'Connell walked around an underground room in a very old Egyptian temple with his wife, Evelyn. She loved everything about Egypt and could read the old languages. She studied the country's temples and its old stories.

Rick and Evelyn met ten years earlier. They found the mummy of Imhotep in Hamunaptra, in the desert. After 3,000 years, Imhotep woke up and tried to kill Evelyn. He wanted to be the king of Egypt first, and then king of the world. But Rick fought with Imhotep and won. The mummy returned to his strange sleep below the ground of Hamunaptra, and Rick married Evelyn.

"Dad! Dad!" a small boy shouted, and ran into the big room.

"What is it, Alex? It's dangerous down here," Rick said to his eight-year-old son.

"But Dad, I saw your tattoo near the door up there!"

Alex looked at the tattoo on his dad's hand. It showed a pyramid with the Eye of Horus★ in the center. Rick didn't know anything about his tattoo. It was there when he was a baby.

"It's the same as the picture near the door! Come and see."

"I'll come in a minute. Now I have to help your mom, and you have to go back up the stairs."

In a different room, Evelyn O'Connell studied a strange picture on a large door. It showed two people in a fight—not

★Horus: the old Egyptian god of the sun; he has the head of a bird.

3

men, but beautiful young women. Evelyn couldn't see their faces, but she thought, "*I know these women. Where are they from? Where did I see them before? Maybe the answers are behind this door.*"

"Rick, come and help me," she shouted. "I want to open this heavy door."

"Yes, ma'am," Rick said with a smile. His wife used her head, but Rick liked to work with his hands. He quickly opened the old door with his knife, and he and Evelyn walked into a dark room. It was full of scorpions and mummies.

"I know this place," said Evelyn.

"You know it from a book," Rick said. "Somebody closed that door before you were born."

"No, Rick. I remember it. I know everything about this room."

Evelyn moved into the next dark room, and suddenly it was 1290 BC. She saw one of the women from the picture on the door. The woman moved—she wasn't dead! She put a box on a table and closed it. Then she looked into Evelyn's eyes. Evelyn jumped, and suddenly it was 1933 again.

"Evy, what's wrong? Did you see something?" asked Rick.

"No, nothing. I'm OK. But look—there's a box on that table."

Evelyn walked to the table and looked at the box.

"The Scorpion King!" Evelyn cried. "His face is on the top of the box. Let's open it."

"Evy, is that a good idea? Wasn't he a very bad man?"

"Yes, but that was in 4000 BC. He's dead. It's not dangerous now. It's only a box!"

Alex was in a big room above his parents. He felt tired because he was bored with his ball game. Then he heard something.

Three men walked into the temple, but they didn't see the boy.

"Why are those O'Connells around here?" the first man, Spivey, asked.

Three men walked into the temple.

"Lock-Nah told us about them. They aren't a problem. We have to get the box," Red, the next man, said.

"But maybe they'll find the box first. Then Lock-Nah won't pay us." The last man's name was Jacques.

"We'll kill them and take it." It was Red again.

Alex wasn't bored now. How could he help his parents? He watched the three men. They went down the stairs.

Two mummies in soldiers' clothes stood in the room with Rick and Evelyn. Rick didn't like mummies. But these two weren't dangerous—they were very dead.

"Rick, this is really exciting! I know the story of the Scorpion King. This is his box! Please, open it quickly!"

Rick didn't like this idea, but he wanted to help his wife. He tried to open the box with his knife, but the top didn't move. Evelyn closed her eyes, and she could see the room in 1290 BC again. Suddenly, she opened her eyes. She put her hand on the box and turned the Scorpion King's head to the east. The box opened easily.

"Look! It's the gold Bracelet of Anubis, the god of the dead!"

Evelyn took the bracelet out of the box and showed it to Rick.

"Stop!" shouted Red. He and Jacques and Spivey walked into the room with guns in their hands. "Give the bracelet to me!"

But at that minute, the floor of the temple began to move. The walls started to fall on them. The three men with guns turned and ran up the stairs. Evelyn quickly put the beautiful gold bracelet back in the box and closed it.

"Put the box in your bag, Rick."

"Let's leave it here," shouted Rick. "It's dangerous!"

"No, it's important!"

Rick put the box in his bag and ran up the stairs with his wife. Alex was at the top.

"Quick! Come this way," shouted Alex.

Rick and Evelyn followed their son to the nearest door and outside into the sunlight. The temple fell down behind them.

"That bracelet *is* important," Rick said. "It has strange powers!"

◆

Red, Jacques, and Spivey returned to Hamunaptra.

Lock-Nah's men were busy that night. They looked for Imhotep under the ground in Hamunaptra. Lock-Nah was with the strange, beautiful Meela, and they had a dangerous plan. Meela had the Book of the Dead. Imhotep gave it to her in 1290 BC when her name was Anck-su-namun. Anck-su-namun and Imhotep were lovers in that life. With this book, she wanted to give life back to the mummy of Imhotep. She wanted her lover back.

"We have to have the bracelet. It will take us to Ahm Shere," said Meela. "And, we have to find Imhotep. With his great powers he can kill the Scorpion King and take his soldiers. Imhotep will be king of the world."

Meela wanted Imhotep's love. Lock-Nah wanted the gold from the pyramid of Anubis.

Lock-Nah looked up and saw Red, Jacques, and Spivey. But before he could speak, the ground started to move.

"It's happening again!" cried Red.

The men stopped working and ran away. Thousands of small black animals came out of the hole in the ground and followed them. When a man fell, the animals ate him in minutes.

"Get some fire," shouted Lock-Nah.

The men stopped the animals with fire, and then somebody shouted, "We have it. We have the mummy of Imhotep!"

Meela carried the Book of the Dead with her and looked down at Imhotep. She put her hand on the mummy's hand and smiled. She wanted to love Imhotep again!

Meela looked at Lock-Nah and said, "Now we can begin."

"Red, give me the bracelet!" Lock-Nah shouted.

"Sorry, boss. No bracelet."

Lock-Nah's eyes looked dangerous.

"We have to have the bracelet. Where is it?" he asked.

"Those O'Connells have it," Red told him.

"Then we will find them. The bracelet is ours!"

Chapter 3   Imhotep in London

The O'Connells arrived at their house in London on a cold, dark night. The sky was full of wind and rain. Evelyn wanted to learn more about Ahm Shere and the Bracelet of Anubis. She found an important book in her office and ran up the stairs.

"Rick, look at this! With the bracelet, we can find Ahm Shere. We can be the first people there in thousands of years."

"I'd like to stay at home for a week or two," Rick said.

"But Rick, Ahm Shere is an important place in the middle of a desert. It has beautiful green trees and blue waters and a wonderful pyramid."

"So, it's beautiful and wonderful. Right? There's nothing dangerous in Ahm Shere. Right?"

"The Scorpion King and his soldiers are there. But they're dead, or asleep," Evelyn said.

"And, when are they going to wake up?" asked Rick.

"The story says they'll wake up in the Year of the Scorpion."

"And, when is that?"

"This year," answered Evelyn quietly. "But it's only a story!"

"I remember the story," said Rick. "The Scorpion King and his soldiers are going to wake up. They're going to kill everybody and everything. Let's forget about the bracelet. Let's leave the Scorpion King and his soldiers in Ahm Shere."

Lock-Nah's eyes looked dangerous.

In the room below his parents, Alex looked into his dad's bag and found the strange box. It looked interesting, so he turned the Scorpion King's head to the west and then to the east. Suddenly, the box opened and Alex saw a beautiful gold bracelet inside. He put his hand through the heavy bracelet, and it closed around his arm. He pulled it, but he couldn't take the bracelet off again.

Suddenly, the boy saw a different world in front of him. It was 4000 BC, and he was in Egypt. He was in the great desert at Giza, and he could see three very large pyramids. He flew over the Nile River and saw the temple of Karnak.

Then, Alex was back in his house in London.

"Alex," his mother called. "Are you OK down there?"

"I'm fine, Mom," the boy answered.

He quickly pulled his shirt over the bracelet. Then, he threw a heavy book into the box and closed it.

Suddenly, the box opened and Alex saw a beautiful gold bracelet inside.

"*I have to get this bracelet off before my mother opens the box again,*" he thought.

"Is everything all right, Alex?" Evelyn asked when she walked into the room.

"Oh, yes! Everything's great!"

In the room above, Rick put clothes into the closets. Then, he heard something in the next room. He opened the door and saw Jonathan, Evelyn's brother.

"That's him!" shouted Jonathan. "*He's* O'Connell, not me!"

Four Egyptian soldiers in red hats and a beautiful woman looked at Rick. They had guns and didn't look friendly.

"Are you O'Connell?" It was Meela.

"Yes. Who are you?" asked Rick.

"My name is not important. Give me the box with the Bracelet of Anubis or these men will kill you and this stupid little man."

"I am *not* stupid *or* little!" cried Jonathan.

"Be quiet, Jonathan. Ma'am, this is my house. You and your friends have to leave now."

"I am not leaving without the bracelet. Shoot them!" she shouted to the four Egyptians.

Rick jumped across the room and took two large knives from the wall. He threw one knife to Jonathan and killed the Egyptian next to him with the other. Rick and Jonathan ran into the bathroom and closed the door.

"What do they want?" shouted Jonathan.

"Evy found an old box and brought it home. They want the gold bracelet inside it. Now, let's go!"

Rick pushed Jonathan through the bathroom window and jumped out after him. They ran out of the yard.

Evelyn heard something above her, but she had problems, too. Lock-Nah stood at the door with three soldiers.

11

"Give me the box. Now!" he shouted at Alex. The boy had the box in his arms.

"Get out of my house or I'll call the police," Evelyn said to Lock-Nah and his men.

"Mom, is that a good idea?" asked Alex.

"I will take the box and kill your son," said Lock-Nah.

"No, you won't," said a man in black clothes. He stood at the door and carried a large knife in his hand.

The three Egyptian soldiers in red hats moved away from Evelyn and Alex.

"Ardeth Bay!" one man said quietly.

Ardeth Bay was the greatest of the Med-Jai soldiers. They guarded the mummies in Egypt all night and all day. The mummies were very dangerous. They had to stay asleep. Ardeth Bay first met Evelyn and Rick in 1923. He helped them win their fight with the mummy Imhotep. He sent Imhotep back to the world of the undead.

Lock-Nah jumped on Ardeth Bay and started to fight. Evelyn took a large knife from the wall and helped the Med-Jai.

"Mom! You're great! You're really strong!" shouted Alex. "How can you do that?"

"I don't know," Evelyn shouted back.

A soldier took the box from Alex. Ardeth Bay pushed his knife into the man's back, and Alex had the box again.

"What's in the box?" Ardeth Bay shouted to Evelyn.

"The Bracelet of Anubis!"

"Get it! Get it now and run!" shouted Ardeth Bay. "Now! Quick! Lock-Nah cannot have the bracelet."

Evelyn took the box and began to run. A soldier stopped her. He carried Evelyn and the box to Lock-Nah's car outside.

Lock-Nah hit Ardeth Bay and the Med-Jai fell to the floor. Then Lock-Nah and his soldiers ran to the car. In the house, Alex sat on the floor next to Ardeth Bay. He called for his father, but nobody answered.

Ardeth Bay was the greatest of the Med-Jai soldiers.

Outside, Rick and Jonathan heard the car start and ran to the front of the house. Rick saw Evelyn in the car with Lock-Nah, Meela, and some soldiers in red hats.

Then, Alex and Ardeth Bay ran out of the house.

"Dad! Dad!" Alex shouted. "They took Mom with them!"

"We're going after her now," said Rick. "Ardeth Bay, what are you doing here?"

"I'm following Lock-Nah and that woman, Meela. They have the mummy of Imhotep in the British Museum."

"What? Why didn't you and your men stop them?"

"The woman, Meela, knows about mummies. She found Imhotep under the ground easily. She is very dangerous."

"And now what's going to happen?" asked Rick.

"They have Imhotep and the Bracelet of Anubis. They will use those powers," said Ardeth Bay.

"They have Mom, but I have the bracelet," Alex said to his dad. He showed his arm.

"They have Mom, but I have the bracelet," Alex said.

Ardeth Bay looked afraid.

"Mr. O'Connell, this is very bad. With the bracelet on your young son's arm, we have only seven days before the Scorpion King wakes up."

"I'm not interested in the Scorpion King," shouted Rick. "I want Evy back."

"The Scorpion King will wake up, and he and his soldiers will kill everybody and everything."

"The end of the world?" asked Jonathan.

"That's right," Ardeth Bay answered. "But one person can kill the Scorpion King and take his powers."

"And that's Imhotep's job?" asked Jonathan.

"Right again. Lock-Nah and Meela are going to wake up Imhotep. He'll be their king. The world will be theirs."

"We have to stop them and get Evy away from them. Get in the car—we're going to the British Museum," shouted Rick.

At the museum, Rick and Ardeth Bay jumped out of the car with their guns and knives.

"Stay here! Watch the car!" Rick shouted to Alex and Jonathan.

He gave the biggest gun to Ardeth Bay. At the same time, the Med-Jai saw the tattoo on Rick's hand. He looked into Rick's eyes.

"I am a stranger from the East. I am looking for an important person," he said, slowly and carefully.

Rick stopped. He remembered a time when he was very young and very sad. He had nobody—no parents, no sisters, no brothers. But he remembered the friendly face of an old man. The old man told the young boy, "Don't be sad. You will have a better life with a happy home one day. And, you will help many people. Remember these words . . ."

Rick remembered the words and said to Ardeth Bay, "I am a stranger from the East. You are looking for me."

"Mr. O'Connell, you can help me and my people. You are a Masonic Templar.★ You have the tattoo."

"I got it when I was a child in Hong Kong. What does it mean?"

"You are a soldier for God. You will help many people."

"No," said Rick. "It's a mistake. You're talking to the wrong man." He turned and ran into the museum, with Ardeth Bay behind him.

It was the middle of the night and the museum was dark and full of strange sounds. Rick and Ardeth Bay found the great Egyptian Room and stopped at the door. They saw Evelyn and the people around her, and watched quietly.

The soldiers in red hats carried Evelyn to the middle of the room. There she saw the ugly mummy of Imhotep.

"Wake up and live! Wake up and live! Wake up and live!" Lock-Nah and the other men called to Imhotep.

A light shone on the mummy's face, and slowly it began to move. First, its eyes opened, then its head moved, then its arms and legs. But they were not the arms and legs of a man. The mummy was not dead, but it was not of this world. It was undead, and it wanted its life back again. It spoke to Lock-Nah and Meela in the language of old Egypt.

"What is the year?"

"Great Imhotep, it is the Year of the Scorpion," said Lock-Nah.

Imhotep laughed and then looked at Meela.

"Anck-su-namun, is it really you?"

"I am here, my love. I am waiting for you," the young woman answered.

Then Lock-Nah showed the Scorpion King's box to Imhotep.

"This is very good!" said the mummy. "Open it for me!"

But when they opened the box, they found an old book.

★ Masonic Templar: an important soldier from old times.

The mummy was not dead, but it was not of this world.

"Where is the Bracelet of Anubis?" cried Meela.

"The boy!" shouted Lock-Nah.

"We will get the bracelet," said Meela. "But look, we have this woman for you. We will watch her die."

Imhotep looked at Evelyn and shouted, "Kill her!"

The soldiers built a fire and carried Evelyn to it. Suddenly, Rick and Ardeth Bay ran into the room with guns in their hands. Ardeth Bay killed two soldiers and shot two other men. They fell into the fire and died.

Rick shot at Imhotep, but guns couldn't hurt a mummy.

Imhotep had a bottle of water from Hamunaptra and he threw some of this water on the floor.

"Come, my soldiers. Move your hands and feet."

Suddenly, four soldier-mummies came up through the floor and stood in front of Imhotep.

"Not more mummies!" shouted Rick. "Let's get out of here!"

He took Evelyn's hand, and they ran from the museum. Ardeth Bay followed them. Alex and Jonathan were outside in a big red bus.

"Where's my car?" Rick shouted at Jonathan.

"A small problem, but we found this," Jonathan said.

"Forget the car!" shouted Evelyn. "Let's go!"

The four soldier-mummies ran behind the bus. They were very fast.

"I hate mummies," said Rick.

Then, one mummy jumped on the top of the bus. From a window, Rick shot into its face. He couldn't kill the mummy, but he could stop it. The mummy looked at Rick with half a face and climbed in through a window.

At the same time, Ardeth Bay saw two mummies at his window and shot off their legs. The legs fell into the street, but the mummies moved down the bus with their hands.

Evelyn saw the mummies inside the bus and shouted, "Turn! Turn!" at Jonathan.

When the bus suddenly turned, Ardeth Bay fell to the floor. The two mummies fell on him. They cut his arms and face with their long, ugly teeth.

Evelyn took Ardeth Bay's gun and shot at the mummies. Their heads flew out the window. Ardeth Bay pushed them through the door, and they fell onto the street.

Evelyn heard a noise above her.

"Turn! Turn! Turn!" she shouted again to Jonathan.

Above them, Rick fought with the mummy with half a face. The mummy was stronger than Rick. It took him in its arms and hit his head on the top of the bus. Suddenly, the bus turned again and Rick had a minute. He got his gun and shot the mummy again and again. But the mummy didn't stop. It threw Rick to the floor. It put one foot on Rick's gun and one on his head.

"Turn! Turn! Turn!" she shouted again to Jonathan.

19

Jonathan saw a bridge in front of them.

"Oh, no!" he thought. "That bridge isn't very high."

The bus hit the bridge hard. The bridge cut off the top of the bus. Glass flew into the street, and the mummy fell to the ground. The bottom of the bus moved quickly away from the bridge. Rick slowly climbed down the stairs and saw his family and Ardeth Bay.

"You're a great driver, Jonathan," he said. "Is everybody OK?"

"We're OK, but I hate mummies!" said Alex. He smiled at his dad, and then sat next to Jonathan, near a window.

A mummy's arm suddenly came through the window.

"Help!" Alex shouted.

Rick ran to the front of the bus, but the arm pulled Alex out of the bus. It pushed him into Lock-Nah's car. Rick and Evelyn watched the car drive away with their son inside.

Chapter 4   A Trip to Old Egypt

Alex was on a train in the middle of the Egyptian desert with Lock-Nah, Meela, and Imhotep.

"Do you have the Book of the Dead?" Lock-Nah asked Meela.

Alex listened carefully. He knew about this important book from his mother.

"Yes," answered Meela. "It will help Imhotep."

A soldier came into the car. "Imhotep wants to meet the boy."

Lock-Nah pushed Alex to the other end of the train and into Imhotep's car.

At the same time, the door of Meela's car opened and Red, Jacques, and Spivey pushed inside. Red carried another interesting old box. It was from the most important museum in Cairo.

"We got your box for you. Here it is. But we want ten thousand pounds for it, not five. We know about the thing inside it," said Red.

"Yes," said Meela. "Imhotep's heart is inside the box. But, he also has to have another person's life. Then, he can live again."

"That means more money for us," Jacques said.

"Ten thousand pounds is not a problem," said Meela. "Come with me to Imhotep's car. He will pay you."

At the other end of the train, Alex looked around the dark car and saw the back of a tall man. But when the man turned around, Alex saw a face with no eyes in it. It was the face of Imhotep, the undead. He felt afraid.

"You have the bracelet," Imhotep began. "You can take me to Ahm Shere."

"But I don't want to help you!" Alex said.

"You are your father's son, I see," said the mummy. "But you have very little time. The Scorpion King is going to wake up seven days after you put the bracelet on."

"I know about that."

"You have to be inside the pyramid at Ahm Shere before the sun shines on it on the seventh day."

"Or, what?" asked Alex.

"Or, you will die. The bracelet will pull your life out of you."

"Nobody told me about that!" cried Alex. He thought for a minute and said, "I only have five more days!"

"Very good. Now you understand, and now you will take us to Ahm Shere. Quickly!"

"My dad is going to get you. Wait and see!" shouted Alex.

Suddenly, Lock-Nah heard Meela with Red, Jacques, and Spivey. He left the car with Alex through the back door, and Meela came in with the three men and the box.

"It's dark in here," said Red. "Isn't there a light?"

Imhotep turned on a light, and the three men saw the mummy. They tried to leave, but Meela stopped them.

"Open the box for the great Imhotep," said Meela.

"No!" shouted Jacques.

But Spivey put the box in front of the mummy and opened it.

White smoke came out of the box. Nobody could see Spivey and Imhotep in the smoke, but they heard strange noises. Imhotep's mummy had its heart back, and it pulled Spivey's life out of him. When Imhotep walked out of the smoke, he was not a mummy. He was Imhotep the Great, a beautiful, strong man with new life inside him. Spivey was on the floor—thin and white and very dead.

◆

Rick, Evelyn, and Jonathan were back in Egypt, too. They were in Cairo. They had to find Alex.

"When Alex put the bracelet on, he saw the pyramids at Giza and then the temple at Karnak," said Rick.

"At Karnak, the bracelet will show him the next place. In the end, it will take him to Ahm Shere," Evelyn said. "But we have to follow him. There's no map to Ahm Shere."

"First, how can we get to Karnak?" asked Jonathan.

"No problem," said Rick. "I know somebody near here. He has an airplane."

In the desert near Cairo, Rick found his old friend, Izzy, in his office. The little man's smile left his face when he saw Rick.

"You!" shouted Izzy. "What do *you* want? You'll get nothing from me. You always bring problems."

"Izzy, we're friends. We have to have an airplane. It's important."

"When I do a job with you, I almost die. Every time! The trip to Alexandria, the bank job, the night with the dancers. You're dangerous!" said Izzy.

"Bank job? Dancers?" Evelyn said. "Rick, we have to talk!"

"Later, Evy. We don't have time for old stories. Izzy, we have to find our son. He's out in the desert. We're going to Ahm Shere. We'll pay you with gold from the great pyramid of Anubis."

"Now you're talking my language. I'll get ready."

But suddenly, they heard the sound of horses. Ardeth Bay and twelve more Med-Jai stopped in front of the building.

*He was Imhotep the Great, a beautiful,
strong man with new life inside him.*

"O'Connell!" shouted Ardeth Bay. "These are my best men. They will follow you and fight the mummy and the soldiers of Anubis. You will not always see them, but they will be near you."

The twelve men went away across the desert, and Ardeth Bay stayed with the O'Connells.

"Thanks, my friend," said Rick. "Let's go. We can't lose more time. Izzy, where's your airplane?"

"No airplane, Rick. I have a beautiful new machine. Look, it's behind this building."

"Izzy! It's a balloon!"

"Yes, Rick, but it can take you to Ahm Shere. Are you ready?"

The balloon moved above the desert, and Rick talked quietly to Ardeth Bay.

"What do you know about the gold pyramid at Ahm Shere?"

"People find the pyramid, and then they never return to their homes. They die at Ahm Shere. But remember two things. First, Lock-Nah and Meela cannot hurt your son because he is wearing the bracelet. And, second, you have the tattoo."

"Is that really important?"

"When you understand your job as a Masonic Templar, you will have great powers."

"Great. But is Imhotep dangerous now?"

"His powers are returning quickly. He will be stronger than the Scorpion King in one or two days."

At the same time, Alex sat on the train with Lock-Nah. He was hot and bored.

"Can I go to the bathroom?" he asked.

Lock-Nah pushed Alex into the dirty bathroom. He stood outside and guarded the door. Alex looked around and saw a little window. He didn't think. He climbed through the window and jumped off the train. When he stood up, everything hurt. But he could see the Temple of Karnak, and he ran to it.

Behind him, Alex heard the train stop. Men shouted and ran

after him. The boy arrived at the temple and ran inside. With the bracelet, Alex could see the Temple of Philae in the desert in 2000 BC. But he returned to 1933 when Imhotep—now a man, not a mummy—stood in front of him with Lock-Nah and Meela.

"You are a very bad boy," said Imhotep. "I will watch you die at Ahm Shere. I will enjoy that. Lock-Nah, take him outside."

Imhotep and Meela had some important work. The two lovers sat near a pool of water in the middle of the temple. They looked into the pool and saw a picture of their life in 1290 BC.

Two beautiful young women fought, and two important men watched them.

At the end of the fight, the winner said, "Nefertiri, you are stronger this time. Maybe one day, you will win." Nefertiri's face was the face of Evelyn O'Connell.

The two lovers sat near a pool of water in the middle of the temple.

"Thank you, Anck-su-namun. You can teach me many things when you are my mother," said Nefertiri. She was the Pharaoh's* daughter, and Anck-su-namun was his future wife.

"Wonderful! Wonderful!" cried the Pharaoh. "Two strong, beautiful women! My daughter can guard the Bracelet of Anubis for me, and my future wife can guard me."

He smiled at the women, but Anck-su-namun did not smile at the Pharaoh. Her smiles were for Imhotep, her future husband's friend and King of the Dead. Nefertiri saw this and hated Anck-su-namun and Imhotep.

Many days later, Imhotep was in the Pharaoh's bedroom with Anck-su-namun. The Pharaoh found them, and they killed him. Nefertiri heard noises and called for help. But her father was dead.

"Run!" shouted Imhotep to Anck-su-namun.

"No," said Anck-su-namun. "I will die, and later you can bring me back to life."

She took the Pharaoh's knife and pushed it into her heart. Imhotep saw her die.

In the temple at Karnak, Meela opened her eyes. She was not Meela. She was Anck-su-namun again.

"Anck-su-namun," said Imhotep, "there is no end to our love. Now we can do anything."

Another person watched the same picture in the pool. Evelyn O'Connell was in the balloon, but she too could see the fight between Nefertiri and Anck-su-namun. She woke up when Anck-su-namun died. She was afraid and told the story to Rick and Ardeth Bay.

"Rick, I was Nefertiri, the daughter of Pharaoh Seti the First. I was a great fighter, and I guarded the Bracelet of Anubis."

"And now our son is wearing it!"

* Pharaoh: the name for an Egyptian king in old times.

26

"Anck-su-namun," said Imhotep, "there is no end to our love."

Ardeth Bay looked at Rick. "You are a soldier for God. You will help many people. You will love and guard Nefertiri and her son. That is your life."

At the same time, Alex sat on the floor of the Temple of Karnak. He couldn't move because Lock-Nah guarded him.

"Please, can I have some water?" Alex asked nicely.

Lock-Nah gave a cup of water to the boy. Then he turned his back and fell asleep.

When Lock-Nah was quiet, Alex built a little temple on the floor. Later that day, he left Karnak with Lock-Nah, Anck-su-namun, and Imhotep. But his little Temple of Philae stayed there.

Two hours later, the O'Connells, Jonathan, and Ardeth Bay arrived at the Temple of Karnak.

"They aren't here," said Jonathan sadly.

Suddenly Evelyn shouted, "Rick! Come and see this! It's the Temple of Philae! Alex is giving us our map. Let's go!"

They returned to the balloon and followed Alex from Karnak to Philae and then to the Temple of Abu Simbel. They followed the Nile River into the center of old Egypt.

"How can we find one small boy in this big country?" asked Evelyn.

"He'll leave us another building," said Rick.

Chapter 5   Ahm Shere

But Alex couldn't help his parents again. He started to make another temple at Abu Simbel, but Imhotep saw it.

"You're a smart boy!" said Imhotep, and then he kicked the temple. "No more buildings! This time, *I* will give something to your parents."

Imhotep looked into the river and spoke in an old Egyptian language. Suddenly, a large wall of water came out of the river.

Izzy drove his balloon above the Nile, between two tall mountains. He heard a strange noise and looked up. But the sky was blue and the sun shone. Then he saw the wall of water.

"Everybody! Help!"

They saw the water, and Imhotep's face was in the middle of it.

"Shoot it!" Izzy cried.

"That won't help," said Rick. "I know this mummy. Turn!"

Izzy turned the balloon right, between two small mountains. The wall of water couldn't turn. It pushed down the middle of the Nile.

After the water went past them, Jonathan said, "People! Look around you!"

They were in a wonderful place with green trees and blue waters. There were fruit trees and flowers everywhere.

"Ahm Shere," said Ardeth Bay very quietly.

Izzy turned the balloon right, between two small mountains.

"It is!" said Rick. "I can see the top of the gold pyramid behind those trees."

But suddenly, they heard the sound of the wall of water again. Before they could move, the water threw the balloon into a mountain. Then it moved away. The five wet people on the ground were tired, but they weren't dead.

"Izzy," said Rick, "we're going to find Alex. Get this balloon ready. We'll have to leave quickly after we get him."

"But Rick ..."

"No 'buts.' This balloon has to fly again!"

"Let's go!" shouted Ardeth Bay.

The O'Connells and Jonathan followed the Med-Jai to a place above the gold pyramid. They watched and waited for Alex.

Imhotep, Lock-Nah, and Anck-su-namun found Ahm Shere that night. The bracelet on Alex's arm showed them and their soldiers the way. Near the pyramid, they saw dead soldiers from earlier times. Nobody came to Ahm Shere and then went home again. It was a place for the dead.

Suddenly, they found an open place in the trees, and they saw the gold pyramid in the evening light.

"Great Imhotep," said Lock-Nah, "can I kill the boy now?"

"I don't want him. He's yours," Imhotep answered.

Alex heard these words and started to walk quietly away. Lock-Nah had his plans for the boy and began to follow him. Then he heard a strange sound in the trees. He stopped.

"Listen," Lock-Nah said. "Is it the dead? Are they singing?"

"Something is coming," Anck-su-namun said.

"Get your guns ready," Lock-Nah shouted at the soldiers.

Suddenly, a man cried, "Help me!"

Nobody could see him. Lock-Nah heard another cry and turned quickly. Something pulled another soldier under the ground. Then everything was quiet, but only for a minute.

A lot of very short mummies came out of the ground. They

fought with the soldiers in red hats. They wanted to get the Book of the Dead from Anck-su-namun, but she and Imhotep ran through the trees.

The little mummies were a problem, but Lock-Nah forgot about them. He wanted to kill Alex. He looked into the boy's eyes, but Rick O'Connell jumped into the battle.

"Alex!" Rick shouted. "This way!"

Rick shot at the soldiers and at the mummies, but Lock-Nah had Alex. Then Rick had some help. Ardeth Bay arrived and fought with Lock-Nah. Rick put Alex on his back and ran.

Ardeth Bay cut Lock-Nah in half. Lock-Nah fell to the ground and didn't move again.

Ardeth Bay ran after Rick and Alex. They found Evelyn and Jonathan, and Alex jumped into his mother's arms. Everybody was happy for a minute.

Lock-Nah wanted to kill Alex.

31

"Dad, you have to help me!" said Alex. "I have to be inside the pyramid today before the sun shines on it."

"Or, what will happen?" asked Rick.

"Or, I will die."

"Let's go! The sky is getting light. We don't have much time!" Rick shouted.

The five people ran through the trees to the pyramid. The short mummies ran after them. Then, they saw the Bracelet of Anubis on Alex's arm and they stopped. The strange little mummies went away, and it was quiet again.

"Rick, look!" shouted Evelyn. "There's light behind those mountains. The sun is coming up. Quick! Run to the pyramid."

Rick took Alex's hand and ran as quickly as possible. Their battle was now with the sun. They arrived at the door of the pyramid and ran inside. The sunlight was a meter behind them.

Rick and Alex sat on the floor and smiled.

"You know, son," Rick said, "life with you isn't always easy."

"Yes, but you like it!" said the boy.

At that minute, the Bracelet of Anubis fell off Alex's arm. Rick threw it away. He never wanted to see it again.

Jonathan and Evelyn arrived at the pyramid. Evelyn looked around for her son and husband. Jonathan looked at the gold. But before they could go through the door, Anck-su-namun arrived at the pyramid. She came near Evelyn, and looked into her eyes. But she didn't see Evelyn—she saw Nefertiri. Anck-su-namun pushed her knife into Nefertiri's heart and threw her to the ground. Then she ran into the pyramid through a different door with Imhotep. They carried the Book of the Dead with them.

Rick and Alex found Evelyn on the ground.

"Dad, is she OK? Is she dead?"

Evelyn opened her eyes. She wanted to say something.

"Evy, don't talk. You'll be OK," Rick told his wife.

She opened her mouth and said, "Love . . . you."

Then, Evelyn O'Connell died.

Imhotep and Anck-su-namun were now in the center of the pyramid. They saw a large gold square on the floor, with the face of Anubis on it. Imhotep walked to the square and stood on the face. Suddenly, the floor began to move, and a loud noise came from under the square. White smoke came out of Imhotep's mouth and ears. Anubis took away Imhotep's powers.

Imhotep slowly turned his head. He looked at Anck-su-namun with sad eyes.

"I am only a weak man now—not a god. I have to fight the Scorpion King without my powers," Imhotep said quietly.

"No, you can't," cried Anck-su-namun. "He will kill you."

"You have the Book of the Dead. You can bring me back to life."

A strange light came out of the floor and moved through the pyramid. The light woke up the Scorpion King and the soldiers of Anubis. Then it flew out of the pyramid and across the desert. Ardeth Bay and the Med-Jai soldiers saw this light and understood. It was the time for their greatest battle.

"Don't go! Please!" cried Anck-su-namun to Imhotep.

But Imhotep smiled at his lover and left her. He walked through the pyramid. He wanted to find his future, but he found somebody from his earlier life. He found Rick O'Connell. Rick ran at Imhotep, and the two men began to fight.

Alex and Jonathan waited outside the pyramid next to Evelyn. Alex cried and cried. Jonathan watched. How could he help the boy? What could he say to him?

"Your mother's in a better place," he began. "The good book★ teaches us . . ."

Alex stopped crying.

"The good book! That's it!" he shouted. He jumped up and ran into the pyramid. Jonathan followed quickly.

They found Anck-su-namun inside the door.

★ The good book: another name for the Bible.

"You killed my mother!" shouted Alex.

"And my baby sister!" said Jonathan. He cut Anck-su-namun's arm with his knife, and the Book of the Dead fell to the ground. The young woman was very strong, but Jonathan was angry. He fought well.

Alex quietly took the Book of the Dead and went outside with it. He stood above his mother and began to read the words in the language of old Egypt. It was very difficult and he read slowly.

"Faster!" shouted Jonathan. "I can't stop this woman. She's going to kill me!"

Alex read the last word on the page. Anck-su-namun's knife was near Jonathan's heart when, suddenly, Evelyn O'Connell was on her feet.

"Jonathan, go and help Rick. This is my fight!"

The two women began their battle: Evelyn and Meela; Nefertiri and Anck-su-namun.

Evelyn remembered her fight with Anck-su-namun 3,000 years earlier. She did not want to lose again. The two women kicked and hit. Anck-su-namun fell to the ground. Evelyn was the winner, but she couldn't put a knife through Anck-su-namun's heart. She couldn't kill another person in that way.

Alex and Jonathan found Rick in a room with Imhotep. It was a difficult fight. They suddenly stopped when the door opened with a loud noise. The Scorpion King walked in! He had the head and arms of a man, but the legs of a scorpion. He looked at Rick and Imhotep with hate in his eyes.

At the same time, Ardeth Bay and 10,000 Med-Jai fought the soldiers of Anubis. The Med-Jai killed the 2,000 dog-face fighters. But it was not the end. Next, 50,000 more Anubis soldiers came out of the ground. A new, more difficult battle began, but the Med-Jai were strong and ready. They had to win this battle for their people and for the world.

It was a difficult fight.

Inside the pyramid, Imhotep did not fight with the Scorpion King. He fell on the floor and cried, "Please, do not hurt me. I will follow you from this day. You are my king."

The Scorpion King stopped and smiled at Imhotep. Then he turned and looked at Rick. Rick waited for him. The half-man, half-animal threw Rick across the room. His back hit a wall. Rick could see fire when he opened his eyes. But he also saw a picture on the wall and a very large, gold knife next to it. The picture showed a pyramid with the Eye of Horus at the center— it was Rick's tattoo! The Scorpion King hit him again, but Rick watched the picture.

"I am a stranger from the East. You are looking for me!" Rick shouted. Suddenly, the large gold knife was in his hand.

But, Rick didn't want to fight with men in red hats, short mummies, Imhotep, or the Scorpion King. He was tired. He was sad. His wife was dead. People wanted to kill his son. He wanted to stop.

The Scorpion King threw Rick at another wall, and he fell to the floor. Then, he saw a woman's shoes and looked up. Evelyn smiled at him!

"Evy?" Rick shouted. "Evy!"

His wife was not dead! Now Rick was ready for the Scorpion King.

Rick and the Scorpion King were in the middle of the room. Evelyn, Jonathan, Alex, Imhotep, and Anck-su-namun watched the two fighters. Rick had the gold knife of the Masonic Templars in one hand, and he danced around the Scorpion King.

The large man-animal hit Rick's knife with his scorpion legs, and it flew across the room. Rick caught it before it hit the floor.

"Do something with that knife!" shouted Jonathan.

Rick jumped up and threw his knife at the Scorpion King. It hit the man-animal's heart, and he fell. Then, the room was full of black smoke. The smoke climbed to the top of the room—and then there was nothing: no smoke, no Scorpion King.

At that minute, the floor opened and the walls moved. Rick and Imhotep stood near a large hole in the floor.

"Rick!" shouted Evy.

"No, Evy! Stay back!" Rick shouted. "Stay there!"

"Anck-su-namun!" Imhotep called. "Help me!"

But Anck-su-namun did not move.

Evelyn ran to Rick. She caught his arm, but he fell into the dark hole. With the powers of Nefertiri, she pulled him out.

"Anck-su-namun!" Imhotep cried again. But his lover was not there. Imhotep looked at the O'Connells with hate in his eyes, and then he fell into the hole. It was the end of a long, strange life.

Anck-su-namun ran through the pyramid into a room with a picture of the Scorpion King on the wall. The floor moved and the walls fell. Thousands of scorpions came from behind the walls. They climbed on Anck-su-namun's arms and legs, on her face and hair. They ate her in minutes.

Rick, Evelyn, Jonathan, and Alex ran through the gold pyramid. The walls fell behind them. There was a strong wind outside. The sky was dark and dangerous. Rain started to fall.

Rick wanted to help his family. The world looked crazy. Where could they go? Then, he looked up. Izzy was above them in the balloon.

"Quickly!" the little man shouted above the noise of the wind and rain. "I can't wait all day!"

The balloon moved down to the ground, and everybody climbed into it. They looked down and watched the pyramid fall into a great hole. The wind and rain stopped, and the world was quiet again. There was no Ahm Shere. There was only desert and sun.

"O'Connell!" said Izzy. "Did you have a hard day? You look tired!"

Rick laughed. "You know: mummies, scorpions, battles. Boring!"

"Dad, look!" shouted Alex.

The wind and rain stopped, and the world was quiet again.

They all looked down at the desert below them. They saw Ardeth Bay and his men.

"Thank you!" they shouted from the balloon. "Thank you!"

Ardeth Bay put his hand on his heart and shouted back, "Goodbye, my friends. I will remember you always!"

Then, the Med-Jai returned to their work in the desert.

Rick O'Connell suddenly felt happy. He remembered Ardeth Bay's words about his tattoo. Maybe the Med-Jai was right. He could help many people. He looked at his wife and son and smiled.

"Let's go home," he said.

ACTIVITIES

Chapters 1–2

Before you read

1 What do you know about Egypt? Why is it an interesting country?
2 Answer the questions. Find the words in *italics* in your dictionary.
   a Do you wear a *bracelet* on your leg or your arm?
   b Is a *desert* dry or wet?
   c Is *gold* cheap or expensive?
   d Is a *king* a man or a woman?
   e Are most *pyramids* old or new?
   f Is a *scorpion* an animal or a flower?
   g Do *soldiers* usually carry cameras or guns?
3 Are these sentences right or wrong?
   a Soldiers often die in *battles* for their country.
   b Kings and *gods* don't usually have much *power*.
   c You can fall into a big *hole* in the ground.
   d *Mummies* work in offices and schools.
   e When you *return*, you come back to the same place.
   f You can see *tattoos* on some people's arms.
   g A *temple* is a kind of store.

After you read

4 Who are they? Name these people.
   a the tall, strong young king from Akkad
   b the great god of the dead
   c an old mummy below the ground in Hamunaptra
   d Rick and Evelyn O'Connell's son
   e three men with guns at the temple near Hamunaptra
   f the three men's boss
5 Why are these important to the story?
   a the Bracelet of Anubis   d the Book of the Dead
   b the desert of Ahm Shere   e the mummy of Imhotep
   c the Year of the Scorpion

Chapters 3–4

Before you read

6 Discuss these questions. Do you think the Bracelet of Anubis will bring problems to the O'Connells? Why?

7 Answer these questions. Find the words in *italics* in your dictionary.
  a Where do you see *balloons*?
  b In your country, who *guards* the most important people?
  c When does a person's *heart* break?
  d Which is the best *museum* in your country?
  e How do you feel when you are a *stranger* in a new place?

After you read

8 Which of these things happen in London? Which of them happen in Egypt? Now, answer the questions in *italics*.
  a Spivey dies.
    How does he die?
  b Alex builds a small Temple of Philae.
    What does this little building tell Rick and Evelyn?
  c Alex puts the Bracelet of Anubis on his arm.
    Why is this dangerous for Alex?
  d A soldier-mummy pulls Alex out of a bus.
    Why does the mummy want Alex and not his parents?
  e Ardeth Bay sees Rick's tattoo for the first time.
    Why is the tattoo important?
  f Alex meets Imhotep.
    Why does Imhotep say, "You are your father's son, I see"?
  g Imhotep, Meela, and Evelyn see their lives in 1290 BC.
    What does this story tell us about Evelyn?
  h Lock-Nah and Meela wake up the mummy of Imhotep.
    Why is this important to the world?

Chapter 5

Before you read

9 Discuss these questions. Do you think Rick's tattoo will be important to the story? Why (not)?

After you read

10 What happens next?

    a "No more buildings!"

    b Their battle was now with the sun.

    c But she didn't see Evelyn—she saw Nefertiri.

    d "The good book! That's it!"

    e Then, he saw a woman's shoes and looked up.

    f "Anck-su-namun!" Imhotep called. "Help me!"

11 Who is it?

    a His face is in a wall of water.

    b He flies a balloon.

    c She pulls Rick O'Connell out of a hole.

    d Scorpions eat her.

    e He thanks the O'Connells and returns to the desert.

Writing

12 You are Evelyn. Write about your visit to the temple near Hamunaptra. Why was it strange and exciting?

13 You are Rick in 1953. Ardeth Bay dies. Write a story for an English newspaper in Egypt about your old friend.

14 Izzy has a lot of old stories about Rick. Write one possible story about the two men before Rick met Evelyn.

15 In 1934, Evelyn wants to return to Egypt and look at more old temples. Rick wants to stay at home. Write the conversation between them.

BESTSELLING
PENGUIN READERS

AT LEVEL 2

American Life

Audrey Hepburn

Black Beauty

The Call of the Wild

A Christmas Carol

The Last of the Mohicans

Mr Bean

The Railway Children

The Secret Garden

Treasure Island

Walkabout

White Fang